GOD
REMEMBERED
ME

GOD REMEMBERED ME

The Miraculous True Story of a POW's Daring Escape in Nazi Germany

JOSEPH BANKS & JERRY BORROWMAN

Covenant Communications, Inc.

Published by Covenant Communications, Inc.
American Fork, Utah

Printed in the United States of America
First Printing: April 2013

19 18 17 16 15 14 13   10 9 8 7 6 5 4 3 2 1

ISBN-13: 978-1-62108-404-4

INTRODUCTION

LIKE MOST YOUNG MEN IN the LDS Church who were coming of age in the late 1930s, I looked forward to serving a mission in some exotic land like my older brother, Berry, had done when he served in Argentina. But my plans turned to dust in 1939 when Germany declared war in Europe and the First Presidency ceased issuing mission calls.

Like so many others, I went to work and eventually married. When America entered the war in 1941, I wanted to serve my country, but I also felt great anxiety about leaving my young wife and unborn child. However, duty called, and I was drafted to serve in the army air corps as an engineer on board a B-17 bomber. How could I know then that this call to arms would lead to the most awful experiences of my life—to scenes of horror that I shudder to recall even today? At the same time, there was simply no way I could predict that these perilous times would also lead to the most inspiring moments of my life.

My training took nearly a year, but when I'd completed it, I was deployed with the other nine members of the crew I had trained with to Oran, North Africa, where we began flying bombing runs against German and Italian targets. Later, we were transferred to Foggia, Italy, where we flew desperate missions deep into German territory, including strikes on the huge oil refineries at Ploesti, Rumania—the most heavily defended targets of all. Enemy fighter aircraft and Triple A (antiaircraft artillery) were a constant threat, and we had many close calls that left our aircraft in tatters, but somehow my life and the lives of my crew members were spared each time. We were grateful because when we completed fifty missions, we would be sent home to become trainers—something we all looked forward to with increasing hope.

As fate would have it, our safety lasted only until we embarked on our 49th Combat Mission. I was to be the only survivor of that fateful assignment when our aircraft was destroyed. I was left the only living witness to the sacrifice of the men I had come to love as brothers. When our aircraft was hit, I parachuted out of it but unfortunately headed straight down into a group of angry civilians waiting for me with pitchforks and anything else they could hit me with because we had been bombing their town. Just when I thought I'd lose my life, not to a wrecked airplane but to an irate mob, two German soldiers saved me . . . and made me a prisoner of war in conditions almost too deplorable to describe.

After nine months in the German prisoner-of-war camp, more than a thousand of us prisoners were ordered to march back toward Germany because the guards wanted to escape the advancing Russian Army. By this point, we were all starving—not hungry but quite literally starving—and it only got worse as we walked for more than 500 miles across the frozen German landscape in the worst winter of the previous fifty years. I didn't see how things could get any worse. . . .

THE MIRACULOUS ESCAPE

I PARTICULARLY REMEMBER FEBRUARY 14, 1945. In addition to being Valentine's Day, it was the longest day we marched. One of the guards told us we'd traveled fourteen kilometers. Six weeks after leaving the prisoner of war camp, we were all very weak from lack of adequate food and drink and from the constant, bone-numbing cold. I think even the guards could see that we were about done in, so we stayed in a barn. It felt like a five-star hotel, and for the first time in weeks, we were able to take our shoes off and air them out. We stuffed them full of straw, hoping it would absorb the moisture and keep them properly shaped if we packed them hard enough. We could also crawl into the piles of straw ourselves, which provided some padding between our bony skin and the ground. Lloyd and I cuddled up to each other with our blanket, and it was the warmest and best sleep we'd enjoyed since leaving the camp back in December. Everyone hated to leave the next morning. I would have preferred to stay there until the war ended, but our guards weren't ready to give up yet.

It was about this point that a guard who was friendly with me said he'd heard rumors about the Americans advancing on Germany in the west. This caused the guards a lot of anxiety. We told them it was obvious the war would soon be over and we thought they should start considering giving up before Hitler had them all killed. I think some of them started to feel the same way because they began treating us a little bit better. Some even asked questions about how a democracy worked and what it was like to live in America, where the government didn't take you away from your family to train you to be a soldier. So much of the time I hated these guys, but then they'd say something like that and I'd think to myself, *They don't know anything about life except what they've been taught by the Nazis.* Then I'd feel sorry for them.

Their anxiety about the outcome of the war caused them to lighten their harsh treatment of us, and they were not as quick to punish a straggler, and they sometimes even offered a hand to help a prisoner up when he fell from exhaustion. The English-speaking guards occasionally gave us snippets of news when they received it. Everyone was growing more and more hopeful that we'd be liberated before long.

The guard I had befriended at times gave me lard out of a can that each of the guards carried on their belt. They told us that a spoonful of lard coated their stomachs and helped them keep warm when food was scarce. Since this particular guard spoke English pretty well, I asked him about his wife and family. He told me he had two sons who had been taken away from him when they turned nine so they could go to a Nazi military boarding school. I thought at the time that the reason Germany was destined to lose the war was that whenever they broke up families, they invited disaster on their society. I think this guard agreed with me, even though he couldn't say too much. Still, it was great to have the guards start acting a bit gentler with us.

Unfortunately, our luck took a turn for the worse when a group of Hitler's dreaded SS troops were assigned to guard us temporarily while some of our regular guards took a few days' leave of absence to recuperate. Our regular guards were, for the most part, ordinary people who had been drafted to serve in their army. While they were loyal to Germany, they weren't fanatics. The Waffen SS, on the other hand, were schooled from the time they were children to be sadistic and mean-spirited savages.

By and large, they were young and well fed, and they were like Hitler's attack dogs. They had been trained to subdue all internal dissent with remorseless attacks on their own people, so a bunch of worn-out Allied prisoners were nothing to them. They were cocky and arrogant and would do anything to provoke us: kicking, tripping, spitting and so forth. When one of our guys had more than he could take and tried to protect himself or strike back, the SS rejoiced. They would beat the offender nearly to death and then stand around and laugh as he writhed in pain on the ground. If anyone tried to get down to help him, they'd kick that person as well. It was a terrible sight to witness, but to resist them was futile in our weakened physical condition. We were beaten no matter what we said or did.

It was a happy day when they got orders to go back to the Russian front, and we almost smiled inside to think that they'd be back in battle. As the SS formed into a column to start their march east, one of our prisoners shouted at them, "I hope our soldiers get you and never let you up again!"

That enraged the SS, and they came back and kicked and hit him in the head and groin until he died on the spot. There was nothing we could say or do. I'll never forget the thud of their guns hitting his body and his moans as he lay dying on the ground. Then there was silence, and we knew he was gone. When the SS knew he was dead, they held their fists high in the air and shouted, "Heil Hitler!" and went on their way, laughing and rejoicing.

It was sickening, frustrating, maddening, and disheartening. Sometimes I wanted to kill them with my bare hands; other times I wanted to curl up and die. But I didn't get a chance to do either since the order came to march on, with the threat of dogs and bayonets to enforce our compliance.

As the days and weeks wore on, our meager diet of nothing more than a single shared boiled potato and a little water took an incredible toll on our health. Everyone I knew had dysentery, including me, and I had to stop ten or twenty times a day to try to relieve myself. Adding to the distress was the fact that we had no toilet paper, so we were forced to use leaves or straw or whatever else we could find, which left our skin raw and bleeding. Fortunately, I remembered something I had been taught at the Boy Scout National Jamboree I attended in Washington, D.C., when I was fourteen years old, and it provided relief in these dark times. In one of the health classes, the instructor taught us that if we ever got diarrhea while out in the woods, it sometimes helped to eat charcoal off the end of a burnt branch or stick.

Since our guards built small fires at night, I asked them if we could have the burnt remnants of their sticks, and they agreed. We'd pass this around the camp and eat a stick or two. Somehow, the charcoal coated our stomachs, which helped relieve the dysentery. It wasn't a cure, but it helped for a while. And though several of the prisoners died along the way and we were all very weak, the biggest motivation that kept us going was the thought that the Americans and English were pushing toward us from the west.

Early one morning, we were walking along a dirt road when all of a sudden some American P-51 fighters came screaming out of the sky at us. Everyone hollered to hit the ground, and Lloyd and I dove for a nearby ditch to take cover. Before it was over, three aircraft strafed us on two different runs, and they killed several of the men and wounded many others. When the skies cleared, we went back to the main group to see who we could help. The German guards were furious about the attack, and they refused to let us go back to help the wounded or bury the dead. They ordered us to march on while listening to the cries of our buddies behind us. It was absolute torture to walk away.

As January and February passed into the history books, our health failed rapidly. When one of the men couldn't go any farther, he'd drop in place, and some of us would put our arms underneath his armpits and lift him into a wagon pulled behind a horse. These were usually the guys who had wounds that hadn't fully healed or who required the use of a cane or walking stick. A brief reprieve on the wagon gave them some time to recuperate, and then they'd half jump, half fall off the wagon and start walking again. Invariably, somebody else needed a spot by then anyway. Eventually, there were too many sick and exhausted men to fit on the wagon, so people would just drop in their tracks. We tried to help them stand up and get going again, but if they didn't make an effort to stand, we had to let them drop, or we'd go down as well. Sometimes the guards just left them where they lay; other times, they'd drag them into a ditch by the side of the road. No one ever told us what happened to them, but I believe they were left to die of exposure or starvation.

With nearly a thousand men marching in a loose formation (the columns were long gone), it was only natural to stay with our friends. Bob, Lloyd, and Roland walked next to me through the whole march. They were my best friends, the best a man could ever wish for. We did our best to protect each other and keep each other's spirits up.

It's sobering to describe how difficult the march was. Everyone was gaunt from starvation and dehydration, and while the guards tried to hurry us along, we staggered more than walked because our legs were so weak. Many of the men spent much of the time doubled over because of stomach cramps from dysentery, so they stumbled because their center of gravity was forward of the natural walking position. For the first few weeks of the march, people had complained about the inhumanity of the Germans in forcing us on a march like this, but after awhile, it took too much effort to talk, so we moved ahead slowly in silence. Occasionally, I'd glance up at another prisoner and see tears streaming down his face because he was so discouraged. A lot of prisoners fell to the ground and would have stayed there to die if the guards hadn't prodded them with the muzzle of their rifles or kicked them until they struggled back to their feet.

It's hard to tell how many lost the will to live as the weeks and months dragged on, but it seemed that the nightly encampment grew smaller with each passing day.

I don't know why I kept walking, other than the memory of my promise to Afton to try to make it home alive. Sometimes as I walked along, I could picture our last days together in Tennessee at the aircraft training camp, and it was almost as if I could smell her hair again and feel the warmth of her hand on my face. On other occasions, I had trouble remembering any of the people at home, and that really scared me. It all seemed so far away, and the only reality I could deal with was the unhappy one I was in at the time. It was at discouraging times like these that I leaned on my friends for emotional support.

There were times when I was so tired I wasn't even afraid anymore. What could the guards do to me? Kill me? That would be a relief. Beat me? I was almost numb from the cold and fatigue. It was a small wonder that the four of us needed each other so much. While each of us became discouraged and ready to give up at some point, there was never a time when we were all down simultaneously. There was invariably someone to prod us along and try to cheer us up. Lloyd had the most trouble, and more than once, I had to help him back to his feet. I remember him sobbing and pleading with us to just leave him where he was so he could die in peace. But we'd made a pact to help each other, so I got Bob or Roland to help me stand him up, and we put his arms over our shoulders to get him going again. When he was finally able to walk on his own, he was so grateful for our help, and he turned sentimental telling us how much he appreciated and loved us. Because he was the one to share my blanket at night, I think he felt closest to me. In some regards, I thought of him as a younger brother who needed protecting and help. Perhaps that's why I cared for him so deeply.

I also turned to my Heavenly Father in prayer nearly every step of the way. There were times when I'd get discouraged and wonder why He was allowing this to happen to me when I'd done my best to live a decent life and stay true to my covenants with Him. At other times, I'd imagine that I was being punished for something I'd done wrong, much like Job's friends tried to convince him that his tribulations were the result of some personal failing on his part. I was trying to comprehend the incomprehensible. I've found that when I'm discouraged, I want to find a reason for it. But there was no good reason for the Germans to do this to us.

The Allies were closing in on Germany, and yet the Germans persisted in marching us from one side of the country to the other. I suspected that they were simply following orders that had most likely been forgotten long ago by those who issued them. Fortunately, God did hear my prayers, and on more than one occasion, I felt Him give me strength beyond my natural abilities. Plus, the very act of praying gave me something positive to think about and brought to mind the scriptural lessons I'd learned as a child in Sunday School and from young adult leaders and from my mother. I felt safe when I thought of home, and it motivated me to keep going, hoping that somehow I might return there one day.

We didn't sing much as the march progressed because it took too much effort. In fact, we didn't do anything we didn't have to. If a button came undone on someone's shirt, he just left it that way because the effort of lifting his arms simply wasn't worth the trouble. We must have looked like a bunch of specters straggling through the muddy countryside. We had started the march in the middle of the coldest winter on record and now found ourselves trudging through the mud of a miserable early spring thaw. As much as I hated the cold, it was easier to walk on hard frozen ground than it was to struggle through the mud. The mud absorbed the energy of my footfall, forcing me to pull my legs up and out of the muck. I've never been so weak or exhausted in my life.

Eventually, as February yielded to March, I found that my earlier confidence of returning home to Afton and my son Randy began to fade. I contemplated just lying down and sleeping until all of this misery was over. When I'd catch myself thinking that way, I'd say a prayer in my mind and ask for strength to keep going just one more day, one more day, and then one more day after that. I didn't get angry at the Germans anymore since it took energy to get angry. I couldn't cry because we didn't get enough nourishment for that. I was so thin that I could nearly wrap my belt around my waist twice, making it practically impossible to hold my threadbare pants up. I couldn't see what I looked like, but if it was anything like the others, it was a disturbing sight. Our beards were full, our clothes were filthy, our stomachs were sunken, and our countenances were haggard. It was a stark contrast to the well-nourished men I had trained with.

Just when I thought I couldn't go any farther, the Germans announced that we were going to camp for a few days in a large, open field surrounded by pine trees. I found a coffee can, and Lloyd, Bob, and Roland made a hole in the can and found some wire to make a handle for it. We then looked around to see what ingredients we could find to make hot soup. There were some roots and greens that had started to grow near a few of the more sheltered trees. The guards gave us permission to build a small fire, and pretty soon we had some steaming water. About that time, one of the other prisoners came over and told us he'd killed a cat, and he offered us some of the meat. It was quite greasy, but it felt wonderful to have the rich taste of the broth in our mouths. The warmth of the fire and water brought a comfort we hadn't felt for a long time. On the second or third day at the camp, a group of prisoners surrounded a horse and clubbed it to death. They offered me a nice-sized hunk of meat, which I quickly cooked and devoured. I was so hungry and in such desperate need of nutrition that that meat may have saved my life. At the very least, it kept a lot of us going for the next three or four days. The camp lasted four days, and we had only the energy to lie around and sleep. It was just what the doctor would have ordered, if there had been a doctor to order it.

We'd covered a lot of territory and were coming closer and closer to the Allied lines. By my estimation based on the map I'd been keeping, we'd marched approximately 800 kilometers (480 miles) in the nearly three months we'd spent on the road. If I had interpreted our direction of travel correctly, we'd marched in an almost diagonal line from the northeastern corner of Germany to the southwestern border. If they kept us marching much longer, we'd actually pass beyond the borders of Germany. Looking at the map, I couldn't understand what their intentions were.

In the evening, we could see the big blasts from the heavy artillery light the night sky as the Germans ferociously defended their homeland from the ever-increasing strength of the Allied onslaught. Sometimes we could even hear the sound of tanks rumbling in the distance as the Germans rushed reinforcements to the front lines. Allied aircraft flew overhead almost constantly. The cold and hunger had taken its toll, and there had been a lot of casualties and deaths. It's impossible for me to accurately estimate the number, since our original group of 1,000 was always spread out for miles along the road or trail, but I'd personally witnessed many men fall to the side of the road, where they lay abandoned until long after we'd lost sight of them.

In a sense, we were all casualties. Our health was poor, and we were nearing the end of our strength. Most of the time, I was hopeful that the Allies would somehow liberate us, but there were also times I felt we'd all die before the Allies would get to us. After all we'd been through, I was almost to the point that it didn't really matter either way. One way or the other, the end was close.

By the second or third day in the large clearing where we'd been allowed to rest, the guards started acting funny, like something was bothering them. I couldn't tell what they were planning or where they intended to move us. Most of the guys were just grateful to have time to rest, but I couldn't shake the uneasy feeling. My fears were confirmed when one of the friendlier guards came to me and whispered that we were going to move out the next day and that shortly after that, the SS were going to assume the responsibility of guarding us. That turned my uneasiness into outright panic. I knew we simply couldn't survive any more beatings from the SS.

Since everyone was lying around in small groups, it was easy for me to approach Lloyd, Bob, and Roland to see what they thought about planning an escape. Bob caught his breath at the suggestion and started outlining a number of reasons it would be too dangerous. If the Germans caught us, they could shoot us, turn the dogs loose on us, or bring us back and take away our shoes, leaving us to walk in the remnants of our socks to wherever they were taking us. The last punishment was exactly what had happened a few weeks earlier to one of the men from our barracks. He died of exposure while walking barefoot through the snow, and there was no reason to think we'd hold up any better.

Roland didn't have to say anything—he just pointed down to his pant legs, where the Germans had painted the letters *PW* on each leg, as well as on the fronts and backs of our shirts. This was to alert people that we were prisoners of war. These large, white letters were so obvious that they stood out even in the dark, truly making us "marked men."

"How," he asked, "could we ever pass through enemy territory undetected?"

I replied that we'd have to travel far off the main roads at dusk or after nightfall. I felt like we could make it without being discovered.

The biggest problem was our lack of ability to travel, given our emaciated condition. I had to admit that as weak as we were, it was really pretty crazy to even think about attempting an escape without reliable maps and food.

But as we continued talking, someone pointed out that if we didn't take the risk, we'd be at the mercy of the SS, who were capable of doing almost anything. Their hatred for the Allies would be at a fever pitch now that the Americans and English were closing in on Germany itself. In spite of the fact that Hitler kept circulating rumors that there was some dreadful weapon in the final stages of development that was powerful enough to destroy Germany's enemies, the only evidence we could see of the wars' progress was a helter-skelter deployment of forces that could only slow the advance of the Allies but not stop it.

So, in spite of the danger, all four of us voted to attempt an escape. We put our heads together, without being too obvious, and came up with a general plan. First, we reviewed the terrain we covered on the last day of travel and came up with a secluded spot about a mile back where we would meet at midnight the next evening. Fortunately, all four of us remembered the place, so we were confident everyone could find it.

We also agreed that if someone didn't make it by midnight, we would assume he had been caught or had changed his mind and we'd head off without him.

A few days earlier, I had traded three of the cigarettes I'd been saving (for an emergency) for a wristwatch from one the guards. I never smoked the cigarettes but found them a valuable commodity to trade for a little food. A watch would aid in calculating both time and direction, since I could compare the position of the sun to the time of day and get a better feel for the direction and distance traveled. It would also make it easier for us to choose the best times to travel to avoid detection.

The next afternoon around 1600 hours (4:00 p.m.), we passed the word up the line of prisoners that we were planning an escape and asked if some of the other men would create a diversion by acting like they were having a big argument. It was risky, of course, to put the word out in case a guard overheard a whispered conversation, but it was the only practical way to slip out of the line unnoticed. In spite of having hundreds of men on the move, everyone was so quiet that any unusual sound could be detected.

The only way we would know if someone was going to help us out is if a fight actually broke out. For the next four or five minutes, I walked with a deep feeling of dread, wondering if a guard was about to come racing back with his rifle pointed at me or if we'd just continue to walk along in silence because none of the other prisoners were willing to risk punishment by starting a fight. I'm sure it was just my imagination, but I could actually hear the sound of my own heart pounding while I waited anxiously to see what was going to happen.

All of a sudden, I heard some shouting up ahead. It sounded like angry voices, but I couldn't tell if it was in English, (which would mean the prisoners were creating our diversion) or just the yelling of a German guard who was angry at one of the prisoners. My heart was pounding so furiously in my ears that I had to focus all my attention on the sound. Sure enough, I heard a heated exchange in English and saw some of the guards running up ahead to see what was going on. My heart pounded like crazy, and I decided it was now or never.

I was the first one to drop out of line, and as I crawled into the bushes, I was sure someone would see me and report me. I crawled as fast as I could, trying to be quiet, praying all the time that the dogs wouldn't hear me and start barking. It was now a matter of life and death, and I almost couldn't believe I was doing it. I didn't dare stand up to run (which is what I wanted to do), since my head would have shown above the brush. Instead, I half crawled and half stooped as I made my way through the forest undergrowth toward our predetermined meeting spot. We'd chosen it because it was in a particularly dense part of the forest, with lots of bushes to hide in. I kept hoping the others didn't chicken out or get caught since I was feeling really vulnerable.

I was so weak from the short rations we had been eating that I traveled for a while and then had to sit down to catch my breath. Plus, I wanted to take periodic breaks so I could sit in absolute silence and listen for any indication that I was being followed or hear if there was some kind of a manhunt underway. Each time I paused, I was relieved to find there was nothing out of the ordinary—just the sounds of the forest and an occasional report from one of the big guns far off in the distance. I'm not sure how long it took, but eventually, I found my way to the small clearing where we had agreed to meet. I sat down, put my knees under my chin, and prayed. I didn't want to look around for fear I would see one of the German guards looking down at me.

I waited for what seemed longer than an eternity and was growing increasingly alarmed waiting out in the forest all alone. But then I heard the sound of rustling leaves. I slipped out of view, hoping it was one of my friends rather than a German guard with his dog. My mouth was dry, and not just from the lack of food and water. I was crouched behind a large bush, trembling with anticipation, when I saw Lloyd stumble into the clearing. His red hair was a welcome sight. I crawled out of my hiding spot and stage whispered, "Lloyd, I'm over here!" He was so thrilled to see me that he threw his arms around me and almost sobbed. "I was so scared, Joe, when I didn't see anyone in the clearing; I figured they'd caught you for sure."

I told him I knew exactly how he felt. It was bad enough to be on the run, but being alone was about more than I could take. I was as relieved as he was to have a companion.

A few minutes later, Roland quietly stole into view, and we gave him a hug as well. The three of us sat down to rest while we waited for Bob to arrive. At first we expected him to show up in just a few minutes, since he would have traveled the same distance we did, but the minutes passed slowly with no sound or sign of him. By this time, the light was fading into dusk, and with the loss of sunlight, it started to get really cold. We all strained our ears to hear any sound of Bob or the Germans. I felt a little safer when total darkness snuffed out the last remnant of daylight because at least no one could see us unless they came directly into our clearing. Of course, the dogs were still a threat since they could probably sniff us out. I personally hoped the guard who had befriended me would cover our disappearance, somehow, when they found we were missing in the evening roll call. Plus, with so many men dropping out of the march because of exhaustion, there was always the hope that the Germans would think we'd simply given up or passed out along the way.

Almost two more hours passed before we heard some noise in the brush. We huddled even closer together and remained absolutely silent. The noise stopped for a moment, and then we heard a timid voice say, "Roland, Joe, are you there?"

I was overjoyed that all four of us had made it safely, and I called out, "We're here, Bob. We're here. Where have you been?"

He choked up as he moved into the clearing. "I had to slip off the trail and wait for the group to march past me once the ruckus was over. It seemed like it took forever for all of them to straggle by. When the coast was finally clear, it was dusk, and I had a hard time finding my way through the brush. I've spent the last few hours just trying to find you. I kept worrying that I was actually marching back toward the prison group instead of toward the meeting spot."

Bob was so relieved to be with us, he sort of slumped right where he stood. I can imagine that he'd used up all of his energy racing back and forth in the darkness. We congratulated him on staying at it until he found us. I loved these guys. They had been my constant companions and best friends since I had arrived in the prison camp. In the previous six months, we'd spent virtually twenty-four hours a day together, and it felt so much safer and happier with them around.

After giving Bob some time to catch his breath, the first thing we did was figure out which way to proceed. We decided to travel at night and lay low during the day to minimize the chance of being detected. That strategy increased the risk, however, that without reference to the sun, we'd get lost and actually work our way deeper into enemy territory. As we were discussing this, we saw the distant sky brighten as an artillery barrage fired into the night sky. A light bulb turned on in my mind. Armies always fired artillery from just behind the front lines. All we had to do was move in the direction of the artillery blasts, and we'd inevitably close the distance to the Allied lines. For us, these blasts became our column of fire, like that which went before the Israelites as they fled from Pharaoh in ancient Egypt.

After trying a number of different traveling positions, we decided we would always travel toward the artillery, marching in single file about nine feet apart from each other. That way, if the enemy spotted one of us, the others would have a chance to duck behind cover to avoid detection. It was the responsibility of the person in the lead position to determine the direction and pace of travel. In practice, it worked out that the leader would walk as quietly as possible for a while then pause to make sure the others were still following. Sometimes the leader would look back and take a silent vote to see what we thought. The final rule was that we were to walk without talking to each other unless there was an emergency.

Occasionally, one of us had to signal a rest break because of the difficulty of walking through heavily forested brush, particularly in our starved condition. Moving through the darkness with only the faint illumination of the moon added to the labor because it was so easy to trip on a root or get slapped in the face with a branch.

Once daylight started to break, we found a place to hide for the day. On that first morning, we were totally exhausted, having spent nearly twenty-four hours awake. Thank heaven, we'd had three days of rest in the large clearing before starting the current march. We each took turns acting as the watchman so the others could sleep. At first I didn't think I could fall asleep, knowing the Germans might be out looking for us, but the next thing I knew, I was being startled awake by Roland to take my turn as watchman. We actually got some pretty decent sleep that first day.

On the second night, when darkness started to fall, we were a little more relaxed about our escape. If the Germans had wanted to find us, they could have used trained dogs to follow our trail, and it was highly unlikely that we could have outdistanced them, given that the guards and their dogs had plenty to eat compared to our meager rations. The very fact that we were still there was a pretty good sign that we'd made a clean break. I'm sure most of the guards assumed we'd dropped in our tracks along the way, although the friendly guards who knew us best would be smart enough to doubt that all four of us, who stayed together constantly, would reach the end of our endurance at exactly the same time. I figured that they would ignore our disappearance out of kindness or, more cynically, out of lack of desire to go out looking for us.

When it was dark enough that we felt safe traveling, the leader from the first night dropped to the second position and the person who had been in the fourth position at the rear assumed the role of leader for the coming day and night. By doing it this way, we each took a turn at the leadership spot. If it turned out later that we had gone off course, we couldn't blame a single individual.

We didn't make a lot of progress the first two nights, just in case the guards had sent someone out to find us. We were also still trying to learn how to find our way in the darkness and establish a routine. It was kind of tough for the person in the lead position to know if everyone else was still following, so we had to work out a series of hand signals to communicate up and down our four-person line.

Our biggest fear remained that we'd accidentally wander back into the hands of the Germans. We all prayed for guidance, asking the Lord to help us find the best course of travel that would lead us to freedom, not farther into enemy territory. As the nights wore on and we became more accustomed to our new mode of travel, we figured out that when we approached small towns, it made sense to take a wide detour so as to not arouse the local dogs and alert the citizens. Sometimes it was pretty tough not to accidentally stumble into a hamlet, since every house was under a blackout order to keep all lights extinguished or at least hidden behind impenetrable black curtains.

On the fourth night of our escape attempt, we found a place we thought we'd be safe, in spite of the fact that there was no brush or branches to cover us. We were so exhausted that we lay down together on our sides (the position where the blankets provided maximum coverage) and did our best to stay warm in the cold chill of morning. The blankets weren't long enough to fully cover us, so we'd pull them up around our neck and leave our feet out. We never undressed or took our shoes off, since we didn't know when we might have to jump up and make a run for it if someone was coming.

As the morning sun started to brighten our surroundings, we all froze in place at the sound of someone approaching. Whoever it was had managed to approach so closely that we didn't dare get up and make a run for it, so we just lay there as still as possible. Suddenly, a German soldier came into view and spotted us immediately. He came striding over to us, yelling something in German. We lay still as if we were dead or asleep. He walked around us and kicked our feet, poking us with the muzzle of his rifle, talking all the time in German. Since none of us spoke German, we had no idea what he was saying. All we could do was pray silently and hope for the best. I imagine that he thought of shooting us just to make sure we were dead, but for some reason, he didn't. He kicked us again and then started hollering as loud as he could, probably for help. We still did not stir.

Finally, he strode off through the bushes, calling out for help. As soon as he was out of sight, we got up and ran as fast as our weak legs could carry us. We didn't know what direction we were going, but we ran anyway. I don't know how far we ran, but we were all breathless by the time Lloyd called out that he couldn't go any farther without some rest. We tried to get him to keep going, and he tried for a little ways, but he almost passed out on us. Even though we were terrified of being caught, we had made a pact to stick together, so we quickly found some thick bushes and trees and climbed in and lay there on our bellies, where we could see anybody who might approach. From this vantage point, we could see that we had actually been paralleling a road German soldiers used on their way to and from the front lines. It was fortunate that none of them had heard or seen us. Given that there was at least one soldier who knew we were out there, with dozens of others nearby, we decided to lay low right where we were until it was safe to sneak farther away from the road and the soldiers.

When it seemed safe to move, we scurried away and traveled in a crouching position until we came in sight of a farm. It was pretty quiet, and it was full daylight, so we hid in some bushes and tried to sleep. After our scare, it was hard to relax enough to sleep, but we managed to get at least a few hours of rest. As it grew late in the afternoon, we decided that someone had to sneak over to the barn to see if there was any food. Out on our own, we hadn't found any food to replace the boiled potatoes that had kept us going as prisoners. After four nights without any food, we were famished, and our energy was fading quickly. We drew lots to see who would crawl to the barn, and as luck would have it, the lot fell to me.

We were hidden in a thick grove of pine trees, but the barn sat in the middle of a large, snow-covered clearing. To improve my chances of getting there without being spotted, I waited until twilight. It was still a bit lighter than I would've liked, but if I waited any longer, the moon and stars would make it even worse. Mustering all of my courage and strength, I slowly and quietly slipped across the barnyard and felt my way to the door. It was closed and did not immediately yield to the pressure I applied. I don't know if it was stuck or if I was just too weak to apply much force, but try as I might, I couldn't get it to budge. Having come this far, I wasn't about to go back empty handed, so I looked around until I found a two-by-four board, which I wedged into a small opening that allowed me to pry the door open. It made a creaking sound, and I winced for fear that someone in the farmhouse had heard it. I slipped quickly inside and stood with my back to the wall just inside the door. I stayed absolutely silent, except for the noise of my heart pounding inside my chest. I strained to hear if anyone was coming but heard nothing. After a while, I let myself relax and catch my breath. Everything we did was an effort, and it seemed like we were always winded. After calming down, I gave my eyes time to adjust to the dim light and then started exploring the interior of the barn. I didn't have a lantern, but there were enough holes in the walls to let in shafts of light from the setting sun that I could see the interior of the barn pretty well. Before long, I found a treasure that at that particular moment was worth more to me than a wheelbarrow full of gold. Off in a corner, I stumbled onto a pile of kohlrabies, which were a cross between a turnip and rutabaga and had a tough exterior and a stringy yellow flesh inside. I was so excited because we could eat them without having to cook them, and they would be relatively easy to carry. I gathered as many as I could in my arms, inched my way back to the door, and pushed it open with my foot. As I stepped outside into the afternoon gloom, I was startled to see a light come on inside the house. I immediately stepped back inside the barn and dropped to the floor. I lay perfectly still as I listened to someone approach the outside of the barn. I prayed and prayed that I could somehow be invisible and that once again I wouldn't get caught. I heard the footsteps walk all around the barn, and just when I thought the door would open, I heard the footsteps turn and head back to the house.

I waited a long time before finally getting the courage to go back to the entrance. I was afraid that they might be waiting just outside the door to clobber me on the head, so I pushed it open very gently with my foot. I didn't hear anything, so I stuck my head outside and looked in the direction of the house. The light went out, so I sneaked out into the barnyard and quietly crossed the open ground back to where the other three were waiting. They had seen the whole thing and were so happy I'd made it without being caught. They were ecstatic to see all the kohlrabies, and we settled back to eat for the next few hours before starting out again. The kohlrabies were about as hard as rocks, and the best we could do was bite a chunk out with our teeth and chew the fibrous flesh until we'd extracted all the juice we could, then we spit out the pulp. They tasted wonderful, and for the first time in months, we were able to savor food without fear of not being able to take another bite. To me, the kohlrabies were like manna from heaven, and I ate until the pain in my stomach started to ease.

It was amazing how quickly the food gave a boost to both my body and my attitude. It was like giving water to a wilting flower. Suddenly, I had the ability to think more clearly, and my legs actually felt stronger than they had in days. It was a great feast in the middle of our wilderness.

After the meal, we tried to catch an hour's sleep before setting out into the darkness. Our plan to walk at night and sleep during the day wasn't working out very well because our anxiety that we'd be discovered made it almost impossible to sleep. In addition to having little food and suffering from the cold temperatures, we were tired most of the time. But in spite of that, we concluded that we must be making some progress since the flash of the heavy artillery was getting noticeably closer and we could feel the concussions reverberate through the cold night air.

Three nights after finding the kohlrabies, we were walking single file through the brush when we came to the outskirts of a very small village. It looked like one of the places we'd marched through while under guard. In their attempt to keep from falling into the hands of the Allies, our German guards had actually marched us past the closest approach, so we were now backtracking over ground we'd covered then. I believe it was Lloyd who said he thought he remembered passing by some apple orchards on the other end of this town, if this was the place he thought it was. We speculated that there might be some frozen apples lying on the ground or maybe even some that hadn't fallen from the tree. The thought of eating fruit was a powerful temptation, so we decided to violate our own rule of always walking out and around a town and instead proceeded carefully and quietly through the town. The forest was so thick in this area that it would have been a lot of work to go out and around, and since there were only fifteen or twenty houses, it didn't seem worth the bother. There was no light anywhere since everyone used their blackout curtains on the windows, and it was late enough that we figured most everyone was asleep anyway. The only danger was disturbing any dogs that might be about, but with all of the noise of the war, they tended to bark anyway, so we hoped people wouldn't pay any attention if they started barking at us.

The place was so small that there was only one road to walk on, so we cautiously proceeded down the single cobblestone lane through the center of the town to reach the other side. On this particular night, Roland was in the lead, followed by Bob and Lloyd and then me in fourth place, also known as the Tail End Charlie position. My natural inclination was to hug the side of the road to stay out of sight, but Roland started straight down the middle of the street. At first I couldn't figure out his reasoning, but then realized that going down the middle of the lane lessened the chance that one of us would accidentally brush up against a house and disturb the occupants. We crept along slowly and deliberately, hardly making a sound, maintaining about ten feet between each member of our team. Roland was a great leader at times like this because he never got excited or panicked.

By the time we reached the middle of the town, we were relieved that no dogs had started barking, and it looked like we were going to make it. Suddenly, I was startled by a voice in the darkness. As I instinctively turned to look, a door opened from a house on my left. The light from inside shone on me, and it was such an unexpected contrast from the darkness that it temporarily blinded me. I stood there like a deer caught in the headlights of an oncoming car, unable to move. Suddenly, a German soldier came striding out of the house straight for me, followed by a woman. Fortunately, the field of light was restricted enough that they could see only me, giving my three partners a chance to take cover. As the soldier got closer, his shadow shielded my eyes enough for me to see a huge German tank parked next to the house. I could see the excited look in his eyes. I stood there, transfixed, unable to move or even make a sound. I didn't know whether to run, put my hands up, or fall to my knees and beg for mercy, so I just stood there. When he reached me, he shouted something unintelligible in German. Before I could think of what to do, I was startled to hear myself respond with a calm, confident German phrase that was obviously appropriate to what he'd asked me. He then replied to whatever I'd said with an almost cheerful, "Ya, Ya, Ya!" Then he put his arm around the woman, turned his back on me, and went back into the house and closed the door. I was so astonished and frightened that I simply stood there with my mouth open. My buddies had seen and heard the whole thing, and when I didn't move, they came out and grabbed me and pulled me behind a nearby outbuilding where we could hide.

The whole encounter had taken only a few seconds. The first thing my buddies asked was, "What on earth did he say to you, and what did you say when you talked back to him?" I told them that I had no idea what either he or I said, since I couldn't speak German. I knew that I hadn't used any of the few German words I'd learned in POW camp, like "Hello," "Yes, sir," or "No, sir." Even if I had, my accent would have been so terrible that a German would have immediately recognized me as a foreigner. Yet whatever I had said had satisfied him. All of us stood there, marveling in disbelief at what had just happened.

Considering that I had been standing fully in plain sight of this soldier, with my straggly beard, tattered clothes, no coat, and bright white letters painted on my trousers and shirt, indicating that I was a P.O.W., it was impossible that he hadn't recognized me as an escaped prisoner. Instead of shooting me or calling for help though, he'd looked straight at me, spoken to me in his native language, listened to my response in his language that I had never before spoken, and had accepted my answer as legitimate. Even if the guard hadn't figured it out, the woman had also stared at me and heard the words that had passed between us. Why hadn't either of them figured out what was going on?

As all of this settled in my mind, I felt a burning in my heart that told me I had been blessed once again and that the Holy Ghost had interpreted what the German had said to me and put the appropriate words in my mouth to respond. I'd been blessed with the gift of tongues. I don't know what those two Germans saw, but obviously, they didn't see the letters on my clothing, though they should have stood out like a neon sign in the bright light that shone through the door. The Spirit may have also changed what they saw. I think in some way, my appearance had been transformed so they had not recognized me.

I've heard it said that for something to be a miracle, there can be no logical or earthly way to explain it. If that's true, then I was clearly the beneficiary of a miracle, and it thrilled me to know God was still watching out for me and that He cared for me. Here in the middle of Germany, with millions of lives in turmoil, He had time to remember me and provide help in a desperate moment. My heart was filled with joy and appreciation, and I immediately testified to the others that it was Heavenly Father who had protected and saved us just then. There was silence for a while as we each thought about it. Then we all agreed that it had to be a miracle. We said a silent prayer of thanks, and even though we should have been anxious to get out of there, everyone stood still for a few a minutes to bask in the glow of the warm feeling that surrounded us.

Unfortunately, moments like that don't last very long, and soon the urgency of our situation forced us to continue our journey toward the Allied lines. . . .

AUTHOR'S NOTE

A Distant Prayer—Miracles of the 49th Combat Mission was first released to the public during the uncertain days surrounding the attack on the World Trade Center on September 11, 2001. With all of the anxiety and unity that followed that awful event, patriotism was honorable and Americans drew closer together, as did the rest of the world, to try to sort out what our new reality meant. Readers of Joe Banks's remarkable story found both comfort and inspiration in the unflinching way he shared the travails of his experiences while serving his country in the dark days of World War II. As Joe recounted a number of indisputable, almost breathtaking miracles that intervened to save his life, many readers found courage to face the trials of this generation, taking inspiration from the knowledge that God watched over Joe in the trials he endured. As one reader wrote, "Maybe if God can remember Joe Banks in the middle of war-torn Germany, perhaps He can remember me." That has been the testimony of the book we wrote together—that God lives and that He is there in moments of greatest crisis.

It was a great challenge for Joe to share these experiences. One night I called his home to get some clarification on one of the chapters I was writing and was touched when his wife, Afton, answered the phone. "I don't know what you asked him yesterday," she said, "but I found him weeping in his office as he sat at his typewriter." Joe had been working on the chapter where his aircraft was destroyed and nine of his best friends in the world lost their lives.

One of the greatest things to come out of the book is that many people who are children of World War II veterans got in touch to tell me that the book provided common ground for them to talk to their fathers about their war experiences. One said, "Dad has never been willing to tell us what happened in the war until I gave him Joe's book. After reading it, he handed it back to me and said, 'If you'll read this first, I think we can talk.'" They did talk, and hearts were opened.

After finishing the manuscript, I asked Joe if he'd ever thought about why his life was preserved when the rest of his crew perished. After all, they were also good men whom God loved.

"I've wondered about it a lot," he replied, "but I honestly don't know."

That's one of the reasons I loved working with Joe—he isn't one to speculate; he simply tells his story the way it happened.

"Well, I've been thinking about it," I responded, "and I think that perhaps it was so you could be a witness to their sacrifice. The scriptures tell us God almost always provides a witness."

Joe pondered that for a moment and said, "I like that. And that's exactly what I am—a witness to the lives they gave up so we can all be free. I guess that makes all of what I went through worthwhile."

On January 17, 2013, Samantha Millburn (our editor) and I had the chance to sit down with Joe Banks and his son Randy to read through the text of this booklet, including the author's note that precedes this paragraph. At one point in the reading, I noticed a tear on Joe's cheek and asked what was wrong. "I'm reliving all of this in my mind as you read the manuscript," he said quietly. For Joe Banks, sixty-eight years had disappeared, and he was once again an escaping prisoner in the middle of war-torn Germany.

We ended the discussion with expressions of our love for one another. Just two days later, on Saturday, January 19, 2013, Randy sent a note to tell me Joe had passed away that morning.

Now Joe's testimony has been sealed. All who read this booklet and all who have read his book have his firm testimony of God's protecting care and of the awesome events he experienced in World War II.

What an honor it has been to help a man as good and inspired as Joseph Banks to fulfill his sacred responsibility to testify.

Jerry Borrowman
January 2013